SONGS
WITH OUR EYES
CLOSED

TYLER KENT WHITE

Andrews McMeel
PUBLISHING®

listen—

all those nights
you spent wandering
little steps outside yourself
were part of a bigger journey

you have always been making
your way back home

there is no one more excited
for your return
than you

CONTENTS

A SONG FOR EVERY SEASON

to the bones in my body:

may you never again
know the crushing weight
of the burdens i have carried
and the hatred i have held
for far too long

repeat after me

         i was
         i am
         i will be

repeat after me

         i am not the sum
         of what i have done
         who i am now
         does not dictate
         who i will become

this morning
i sat down to write a haiku
it started out as

you and me and you
and me became us and we
and have i said i

love the sound of your laughter
over our sunday morning shows
and the color of your voice
as you draw out my name?

because i do

and i've never been good at poetry
and i'm still not certain how to
write a haiku

but i do know there are
not enough syllables
to spell out
how much i love you

i love you i love
you i love you i love you
i love you i love

you

are my every moment
my every hour
my every day
my every season
and i know this isn't poetry
and it's certainly not a haiku
it's just all the things
i needed to say to you

in the field of quantum mechanics there is something called quantum entanglement. it is what happens when two particles interact, vibrate in unison, and are separated. they remain connected by something that defies logic, something science has yet to explain. if one particle vibrates, no matter the distance, the other particle reacts in unison. even if there are oceans between them, even if there is a universe separating them.

before time we were just a dense collection of particles confined to a space smaller than a proton, interacting and moving in unison. an event occurred that rapidly expanded the particles and created the universe. there is no reason to believe the particles ever lost their entanglement.

now, when i say i am drawn to you, that i feel i have known you since the beginning of time, know that it's beyond my control. know there are particles that compose me, my very fabric of being, and inside of you are the particles mine danced with millions of years ago. i've spent an eternity chasing that part of you.

you are a
symphony
of stardust
and you were
born to shine

what if i told you
that i've been charting the oceans
in all the smiles you have given away

that i've created monuments
from all the tears you've cried
to false idols who stole
the forever from your lips
leaving you with their goodbyes
pressed to your palms like stigmata
and a mouth full of promises
stuck between your teeth

would you believe me
if i said you were three shades short
of all my favorite hues
and that i've been trying for years
to pick words from my garden throat
in attempts to explain to you
all the things i can't explain

or what if i said
i have nothing to say
other than i love you
in the simplest of ways

when you doubt
the brilliance of your shine

i will take you
through my darkness

i will show you where
you shine the brightest

you are not just poems on a page
or the words people chew on
stuck between their teeth for days
you are not the pieces
or the prose
       the lines
       limericks
       verses
or hymns
you are not just the ballads
burning bellyaches in the bodies
of thousands of strangers
who felt they could stomach
what you had to say

no, you?

you are so much more
you are every sonnet sung in
opera houses that show their teeth
and flex their frames
at the sound of your name
you are a talent beyond measure
a monument made mortal
all flesh
       and bone
            and blood
but what lives inside of you
and crawls through your lungs
in a symphony of sound
from the center of your storm
every time you speak
i cannot say

no, you?

you, my dear,

well you're a goddamn miracle

don't look
to the sky
for fireworks
when you can
watch them
light up
in the eyes
of all the people
passing by

how could you ever doubt
the ways in which you exist

do you not hear the thunder in my voice
and feel the electricity on my lips
when i speak your name

do you notice the way the earth
shakes
       and quakes
                and
splits at its seams
when you wake every morning

or feel the way the winds
always push against your back
dance in your hair
and linger
for the chance to carry your next breath

on days you do not feel you are enough
listen to the silence
the steady cadence
and constant reminder
that no force ever created
is greater than the one
that exists inside of you

on average we speak around 13,000 words per day. how many of them did you use to congratulate, compliment, or encourage yourself? to say, "i know you're doing the best you can"? my guess is probably not enough. so tonight, when you've only got a handful left, remember to say "i love you" to the one person you probably don't say it to enough.

what created the stars
also created you
do not ever doubt
that you burn
just as brightly

come to me with everything you have ever hated about
yourself—the way your hair parts, that crooked smile,
the freckles behind your ear, and your bruised knees.
bring all the lovers still lingering on your lips like a bad
pull of whiskey or the last tobacco of your cigarettes.
show me all the dark places, all the parts you keep hidden
away, all the messy, fucked-up "there is something wrong
with me" parts you wouldn't dare show anyone else.

come to me with all the salt you've ever tasted, all the
tears you have ever cried, the apologies you ever gave,
the belly full of contempt for things you will never be.
i promise to open you gently, explore the morbid, sad,
strange dusty corners of your soul. i will plant kisses on
all the self-inflicted wounds inside of your chest, from
nights you were too careless with yourself. i will let
you know those parts of you are just as beautiful as all
the sunlight you have been chasing and waiting for.

never apologize
for burning too brightly
or for collapsing
into yourself
every night

that is how galaxies are made

do me a favor—

close your eyes and count to all the colors
you've been missing in every arizona sunset
and california sunrise
there are mauve mallows and cerulean baby moons
pushing up through the sinews of your flesh
tell me that their roots have taken hold
tell me that you've sprouted flumes
from your wrought and writhen limbs

can you feel the dahlias and daisies dancing at your feet
their spindle stems tickling between your rooted toes?

breathe in the vetiver and salty brine and petrichor stones
you've forgotten to take note of the ocean
the mechanical whales and serpentine seraphs
molded from the clay beneath your fingernails

you are just stardust and fresh water
                                    little human
exploring all the places from which you came
let the moon bathe you and the sun undress you
take the time to plant your seeds in elements man can't create

there's a world you have forgotten to notice
moments you have missed
that only exist when you close your eyes

this is the sad truth—

      we are all going to die

and all the i hate
      i love
      i want
      i need

you

have ever said in your life will fade
burning light from a failing body
and the blood in your veins
the collagen in your bones
and breath of your lungs
will return

      flecks in the dirt
      songs in the wind

but the parts of yourself
that you gave away
in soft smiles and gentle hellos
that changed the trajectory
of another person's life
those will stay

and in the pulse of the earth
you will remain

give me what burdens you
i will bury it inside of me
and when the roots take hold
             my body fails
             and i finally fold

out of the remains
only beauty will grow

you are a world
unto yourself
just waiting
to be formed

this morning i woke
with my ear pressed
between shoulder blades

every inhale
every drum

    every pump

                thump

of your heartbeat
said one thing—

    home

    home

    home

i choose you
again and again
at the start and finish
of every single day
no matter the season
no matter the age

i choose you
to struggle and succeed with
to fight and wake up with
to love and grow old with

i choose you
knowing there are still trails
we must travel
knowing there are mountains
left to climb

i choose you
to always be by my side

the universe
at any given point
in any given time
is expanding

      infinitely

in all directions

so trust me when i say
you are the center of mine

she was a ballet of places
she had never been
maps strung out
across her skin

in meters and miles
she measured the minutes
it would take to get from point a
to points she knew she had to b
points she could not wait to c

and all along i was just hoping
they all led her back to me

she woke up
every morning
with the option
of being anyone she wished

how beautiful it was
that she always chose
herself

do not tell me about the cities
i have no use for them
tell me about the oceans
and how they've changed in you

        about lemongrass
        and the summer storms

coming in off your shoreline
about the waters that have
carved canyons in your bones

do not tell me about the buildings
i do not care for their heights
tell me about your first breath of foreign air
about the history that fills your lungs
tell me about the memories you made
in languages you can't even begin to understand

do not tell me about the mountains
instead tell me how they were formed
tell me about the head-on collision
of tectonic plates
about wrinkles along the fault line
about pockets of earth
that folded up into the sea

tell me about the rains that washed
and wore you down
about the travels you took
to find yourself
and how you left a part of you in every place
yet somehow always came back more complete

the earth did not ask

        why me?

when her plates shifted and
her fault lines stretched and
her contours
        pushed
        and pulled

she knew that with any change
there was bound to be some pain
but that is what it takes to grow

and you?

you are her salt and
you are her sand

there is nothing about you
that was meant to be small

you are a world unto yourself
just waiting to be formed

no amount of darkness
can drown out our light
if our light
has been lit within

have you ever stopped
looked yourself in the eyes
studied the lines that crease
your once-smooth skin?

have you considered the stories
that exist in the folds of your palm
as you press them against another's?

you should

you are a fucking miracle

the most beautiful sonnet ever sung
a masterpiece unto yourself

there has never been a story
written or told
that is greater than you

do not ever let another person
play a part in telling it
if they cannot appreciate
just how breathtaking you are

one day
you are going to fall in love
and instead of breaking
                    like before

you'll find you fit perfectly
into all the fractured parts
                    and rusted
                    worn-out spots

you'll realize you are more beautiful
than you ever could have dreamed
more stunning
than you ever imagined

you see
          little love
the universe always knew
just how flawless you would become
when you finally took the time
to fall in love with yourself

we need to love
and after we have loved
love again

because the next pair of hands
that fit perfectly
in the empty spaces of our own
may be the ones that help
build us up and
hold us together
rather than tear us down

a mouth
full of muted
magenta—

      heather hiding inside
      periwinkle petals

a lilac sprouts
to hear your laughter
all of the earth

      wilting
            withering

      blossoming

inside your lungs

i hope you know
that it takes time to grow
that there will be days
when the suns fade and
the moons are slow to rise

nights where your heart will ache
and the stars forget to shine

there will be afternoons when
the flowers won't bloom and
the birds don't sing and
the cloudy skies remain just that
cloudy skies

but there will be mornings
when you wake up and
your limbs have stretched
your heart has grown
and the cold has left your bones

there will be a new emptiness
created to carry the memories
more space for the ones you love
more room for new cities
warm smiles
and the glow another's name can bring

know that the voids are
simply places for something
more beautiful to grow

the earth experiences
roughly 20,000 earthquakes a year
or just under 55 every single day
this after living to be millions of years old

so why do you hold your head in shame
as you grow and change?

you were made to be fractured
look at your scars

your fault lines were designed
to collide
and retract

look at your knocked knees and stretch marks

you don't need to worry about
getting it right

you just need to worry about
giving your best

knowing at some point you'll get it wrong

remember—

the world is still forming
and you are doing the same
let everyone remember you
for how the ground trembled
beneath your feet

the love
we were promised
in fairy tales
was never something
for us to find

it has always
been something
for us to create

it's a lot like sunday mornings
and cup rings on the coffee table
and cartoons in the afternoon
and "what do you want for breakfast?"
and "i dunno, what do you want?"
and finally deciding on catnaps
in each other's arms

it's a lot like drowsy eyes
and tired sighs
and the space between my fingers
where yours always seem to be
pulling me back to bed saying
just fifteen more minutes
and me pretending you really meant
forever

and it's a lot like 4 a.m. when no one is awake
and laughing until your sides ache
and humming lullabies until we fall asleep
and waking up to dreams come true
and waking up right next to you

it's a lot like tousled hair
and smiling with your eyes closed
and rosy cheeks
                back porches
                bare feet
                fireflies
and fairy tales

it's a lot like sweatshirts too big
and chicken soup when you've got the flu
and how we both have it now because
i can't stand to be away from you

it's a lot like drowning in your bedsheets
or drowning in your eyes
or just drowning

it's a lot like falling in love

it's a lot like me and you

when i am old
weather worn
and gray

i want to fill my lungs
with your perfume
and hear your laughter
echo through our home
as we dance alone
in our living room

drunk off wine
still madly in love

THE INTRICACIES OF ODD NUMBERS

some mornings
i feel so strange
i just come home
and watch myself sleep

i am writing a manual—
                    a guide on how to find yourself
                    when you are both the search party
                    and the sea

and all you've got is
                    courage and a compass
                    a head full of stars
                    a handful of question marks

and an old map
from the back of a cereal box
that reads x marks the spot

imagine if i had hands
that could cradle the sun
or a mouth that could devour the moon

imagine if i was a promise that could be kept
a forever that did not end

my biggest fear is that
when i finally find myself
i'll still be who i am

somewhere
there are minke whales
singing songs inside my belly
breaching the meniscus
with andesite eyes

somewhere
there is seafoam and driftwood
lapping against my skin
hello and goodbye
floating in bottles
love notes to faraway friends

please
remember me in
vetiver notes and
pearlescent chords
remember me
in measurements of the moon

somewhere
the wind cracks and cries
the rain comes in at odd angles
tides rise and swell
crowding my throat
with sand and gravel

somewhere
your name is stuck to my tongue
beating against the backs of my teeth

somewhere
a canary cries
a lighthouse fades

i dream dreams where i am
floating in achromatic ponds
i am cradled in the womb of this earth

somewhere
my last breath is leaving my body
and i do not feel a thing

i think about my funeral
and how i would like to live forever
about mourning doves
the first fall of winter
and how none of this is fair to me

about saucer-eyed frogs and the
songs they sing to the firefly kings

about pumpkin carriage kingdoms
and the fairy tales i will never live
as i count down the notes of autumn
that the flowers play each night
as they stand tiptoe tall like the trees
pleading for spring to come back home

about moon stones and
how the stars' glow must weigh
heavy against the paper clouds

and how i will live forever

i am 26 and i've already got decades of mistakes
laying in the lines of my face and centuries' worth
of regret stained in the creases of my palms
i've folded up people like wilted leaves and
tucked them beneath my skin
because i don't know what to do
with the care i am given or the love i am shown

so

i have hidden them away for all the rainy days i see
on my horizon, cumulonimbus clouds accumulating,
waiting for me to fall to my knees and say,
"today, today is the day i am finally done"

i used to be a seraphim harvesting sunsets
from the moon-bone graveyards
hidden in the dimples of the stars
i would hang them like wind chimes just to
hear the sound of every dream ever cast out onto
their tales of light every lonely, empty night

i used to stand on the shoulders of giants and
hammer out the dents my mallet hands created
when i was too boyish and rough with the people
that raised me

there used to be magic inside of them
there used to be magic inside of me

i used to say, "i'm never going to grow old and talk
about what i used to be" because i believed the
future held so much more promise for me, but with
every step forward i realize i am much closer to the
end than i am to the beginning

lately my heartbeat has been
        more diminuendo
        than crescendo

with each pump
a little more loose
and lazy
than the last

there are birds outside my window
dreaming of oceans and treetop canopies
i dress them in scarlet and name each one pastel
while they sing me lullabies and tell me stories
about what the moon does when
no one is watching her

their cat claw feet are too fragile to hold
their frames as they stand in vain
stretching tiptoe tall for clouds
they will never reach they tell me
about the songs from centuries ago
still carried in the winds
and empty-nest syndrome
and how broken hearts
and broken homes
both begin with i love you
and end in goodbye

i tell them—

quiet your songs and rest your wings
you will never fly
                           little cagelings
your cement-filled lungs
and feathered frames are
too heavy to call your own
hollow out your bones
and dry the regret from your eyes
some of us were never meant
to have such bold dreams

tonight
i am harvesting the sunset
and teaching the flowers to speak
in binaural beats
to the moon-soaked trees
through static teeth

tonight
i am comatose
a body

       blanched

bled out

i am oxidized
i am fusible

i am auroral light

when they find me i will be
a silhouette laid to rest

sepals
       pressed between palms

petals
       folded up to fit
       into places i do not belong

such is the fault of man
that we can speak
and ask others to listen
but we cannot listen
and ask others to speak

today the silence inside of me is a low hum
power lines banging between synapses
all static sound and shuffling feet
i can feel my memories moving in retrograde

today i am 28 and more aware than ever
that i will never know all the dreams i once had
time comes through in the shiest ways
reduced melanin and deteriorating collagen
i have come to realize why homes settle and sigh
when the weather changes and we are asked
to withstand another storm on our own

my freckles have faded
the fire inside me has too
no longer can i hold the moon
until she sees her sun
the stars seem so far away

28 and i am still learning to see
all the shades that depression shows up in
it used to be only darkness i was afraid of
but now the light holds unfamiliar truths
that i am not as invincible as i once was

now my days i spend more time listening
and less time writing
i thought by now that order
would be the other way around
i thought i'd have everything figured out
and maybe my voice
would matter more than it does
but i sound just like everybody else
a soft plea against the hurricane

for 28 years it's been
the same conversation with myself

just hold on—

even the most
violent storms
eventually die

even the
dimmest lights
have a chance
to shine

there are lesser men that live inside of me. i know. i have been them. there are lesser men that live inside of me and i know because some days that's still who i am. a few steps short of the finish line and a few lines shy of the perfect rhyme. i am not made of steel and stone as once thought, though i warp when the pressure becomes too much for me to bear and fractures form at my fault lines just the same.

there are lesser men that live inside of me and i have come to outgrow them, let them lie dormant beneath the buildup of sinew and scar tissue and mistakes i made and knowingly repeated anyway. if a little sunlight and water is all that is needed to grow then these desert towns should have made me a man long ago, but i am withered from exposure and brittle boned, though still standing. i may not stretch as tall as the trees, but we breathe just the same. my limbs ache just as theirs to hold the skies in my hands, to know i am supporting something greater than myself.

there are lesser men that live inside of me and i have learned to let them go. their wounds are no longer my own and their mistakes are ones i have repaired. my hands don't quite know how to heal all that i touch, but trust i am learning. being born abandoned and a bastard was always my excuse to hold things too tightly, touch too roughly, to claim violence was simply how i learned to love. and there is nothing left inside of me. not the rotgut and rain in my throat, not the contempt for things i will never understand, not the roots dug deep into barren soils. no. i have learned to grow in darkness and used it to show others their light. i have found

there is as much purpose in the silent and stagnant hum of days lost to depression as there is in the days where the highs are too high, where no amount of gravity can tether me from getting lost in what this world is.

there are lesser men that i am better than. over ten thousand stand before me as i face the mirror every day. a soft plea to the fine lines of my face, the scars that have stretched and grown with my skin, the gray flecks of my hair. a soft plea to those that stand before me. please, make me better than who i am.

you were an astronaut
the day the clouds
were pulled from your chest
you fell from the sky
into munsell's color wheel

what is the code for seafoam?
for the parliament hill fields that coat your skin?

you live through a kaleidoscope
of amaranth-skewed hues

i watched you sink the sun into the ocean
and paint fire on your cheeks
the stars danced wildly
the mountains rose to their feet
even the tulips shed their tepals
and called out your name

you were a thousand spiders
scattered from their nest

drink your sherry
dance at the feet of apollo
do not mind what other people think
they only exist inside your head

you are too many moon-soaked bones
folded up to fit into places
you do not belong

last thursday you ate sixteen jelly beans
and refused all the purple ones

with a mouth full of starch and glucose
you told me about the car accident
your parents were in when
you were in 4th grade

how sometimes you lie beneath the moon
and feel your frame
flex on impact

i ask you how it feels to bend and never break

last autumn you colored your hair indigo
and left a ring around the sink
when you ask me what i think about
when the house is quiet at night
i say things like

> porcelain or
> linoleum or
> primrose and
> aubergine

instead of

i am remembering the contours of your curves
and how gravity has made you just so
how i am tracing constellations between your freckles
and memorizing where your hair
parts on the top of your head
i am thinking about crushed glass on the ocean floor and
how you look getting up in the middle of the night
wearing nothing but moonlight

i am listening to your voice and the sound of rain
and thinking about how i am falling in love with you

or sometimes i say

       i am writing a poem about you
       that i won't ever remember

the world needs more men like me
men made of granite
sediment

stacked and
        stacked

worn and
        weighed

until we are cold stone
hands like tectonic plates
shoulders sprawling out
in a mountain range

until we are land holding back
the oceans
        shorelines made to
withstand the waves
and exhaust the raging tides

the world needs more men like me
men made of granite
with hands made to start earthquakes
a heart divided by lines
i wonder which were my fault

the world does not need men like me
men who think their rough edges
do not need to be rounded out
men who think they are granite
perfect foundation for

      roof and
      wall

men who do not realize
they are really the storm

i've had some days, you know

days my blood just can't seem to stay
in the hallways of my veins, days the
pressure folds me up and the doubt
fills my lungs and stifles my voice

and i've gone through some times

times i picked the gravel from my
knees and wiped my bloody palms
across my shirt, times i coughed up
the dirt that was kicked in my face
times i had to eat it

there have been some nights, too

nights i paint the walls of my ribs
with all the hate i have for myself
nights i fail to be the man my
shadows cast, nights i sleep with
my demons and wake up to my
past, nights i feel are my last

but i get up, always

because i was made for this

this is my final sonata, a piece i call "becoming a gentleman without starting forest fires every time you abandon love you never really wanted in the first place." it is played out in the cemetery i've constructed inside of my chest, on the tombstones of every romance i was too selfish to let leave, buried beneath the river waters running through my rotted limbs, well below the shipwrecks and skeleton bones i have used as stepping-stones trying to hang my white flag surrenders from every memory i've held on to for too long.

so here it is, my soliloquy, the stage for my final plea where i will speak into every empty room still left inside of me, reciting every reason i need you to believe in me, to believe that poets are more than dreamers and in all the dissonance and discord i have created a masterpiece strung together with all the words you ever loved, laid on velvet and plucked from velour. i need you to know that they were written for you, that they mean more than the sweet nothings i have given away far too freely to all the stars as i dream at night.

know that i have been biding my time, contemplating the color of your echoes and the sound of the ocean as it gets caught in the currents of my rattle-coin throat, and how my complexion will wear against her waves as i stand in the wake, pleading for them to bring me different endings to all my favorite stories.

please, let the hero die in the end. let the broken hearts never mend. let it hurt in all the old wounds, sutures we were never strong enough to pull. explain how love really is—a series of incredible highs and disappointing lows punctuated by expectations that this time, this time, everything will be different.

ON NIGHTS YOU DO NOT
REMEMBER HOW TO SING

what a beautiful heartache
that i'm still falling in love
with the parts of you
that i never got to know

you are the fever
that never broke

the name stuck
in my throat

you are every letter
of every word
in every poem
i ever wrote

it is not that she loved his laughter
any more than the rest

or that the draw of his skin
pulled more neatly across his chest

or that his kiss did not carry the taste
of all the love he had given before

it's that in the silence
with still breathing
and hearts beating
he whispered a song
and played a melody

that only she could sing

do you remember 2 a.m.
singing taking back sunday
as the bars closed?

remember the last days of summer
moving all your furniture
and microbursts
and monsoons?

or how we'd make small talk
sitting in empty parking lots
wondering why we ever had to
say good night?

the first time we kissed
it was vetiver and petrichor
you had september on your lips
i had forever on mine

i knew with you
i could make that promise
and it would never be a lie

this is the 4th time this week
we've had this talk and
your knuckles are ivory white
and the seat belts are tethers
to this speeding steel cage

i remember the faint sound
       of purple
             and lemongrass
when we met

i remember your body
lying against the silence
and how you moved
in retrograde

before we struck the median
i saw the tears
      well
           and collapse
in your eyes

i felt myself
reaching for you
in different gravities

what they don't tell you
is sometimes love
is a single serving
with a best-used-by date

and that the sweetest kinds
come in concentrate
only ever meant
to be diluted down
and used up

until there's nothing left

to me
　　　　you'll always be

the rising suns
the sinking moons
and all the stars
that come between

the sound of rain
and river stones
the warmth of my sheets
the ache in my bones

and
i'm still dancing
with your ghosts
and sleeping
with your memories

i visited all the old coffee shops
haunts we used to say were "our spot"

the rickety bones of all the ghosts
were still there
greeting me like old friends do

i held them tightly against my rib cage
and i swear
i could still feel the love we had
hear the gravel in your voice
see your river-stone eyes
smell the oceans and sea
still clinging to your skin
and taste my name on your lips

you know
it's a funny thing
you say you've moved on
but i still find parts of you
in the dusty corners of this town

and when i opened myself up
dug out all the decay and rot
i had let grow over the last year

there you were
hiding
an infant inside of me

heartache is
imagining someone else
wishing you good night

i've been thinking a lot about
rainy days and the scent of
patchouli and how to find the
integral of the square root of
tangent and what the people of
pompeii felt in the last
moments before vesuvius
decided to take her revenge

and you

i've been thinking a lot about you

i know there are equations
that will help me understand
what has come to separate us:

> - time
> - distance
> - i love you's, whispered

from someone else's mouth

but i'm still working out the
median of forever and how 1 + 1
does not equal us, besides

i have never been good
with numbers and i

have never been good with you

i'll always miss you
but not as a whole
i still find pieces of you
wherever i go

to me
    you'll always be

laced patterns
on moonlit skin
tousled hair
and tangled limbs
heavy sighs
and soft moans
teeth-mark i love you's
left on collarbones

2 years
14 days
8 hours and
53 minutes ago
it was 68 degrees and you were
3 feet and a table length away from me

sometimes it's the tiles in the grocery store
sometimes it's the temperature at night
sometimes it's the rain against my windshield

and some days it is everything
that reminds me of you

i write equations like:

> the great barrier reef is actually 3,000
> individual coral reefs, 300 coral cays,
> and over 600 islands

> the human brain can store 3 million
> hours of memory

> i have walked 2,816 miles since we last spoke

> solve for x where x no longer equals you

i think in terms of numbers because
it gives me a way to measure
when i will stop missing you

i just need to figure out
if it will be calculated in
        miles or
        days or
        people or
the empty space left between my fingers

you know
there's still days
i harvest the sunset

       and miss you
in quarter moons

days i count
every single star

       and wonder
which one did you
pin your wishes to?

to me
      you'll always be

empty sheets
and lonely rooms

foggy windows
and sunday afternoons

i remember
where you fit in my arms
and how your voice sounded
as you spoke softly to the rain

the color of your smile and
the scent of your skin

i remember everything
but i can no longer remember you

and it's funny
how after you left
all the parts that i still love
remained

i do not know
what i lost when you left
when i lit too many fires
in the hallways of my veins

the human body is not a safe place
to house my emergencies
and you did not ever ask
to be my waiting room

lately
i've been counting all the colors
from one to forever
tying them off to memories

you were always
my favorite shade of summer
and if anyone ever asks
what my favorite number is
my reply will always be

you

here are all the things i never said

that you remind me of
        lilac notes
        and petrichor

that you've always been
four shades shy of my favorite hues
and when autumn wanes
and gives way to winter
i think of blue spruce splintering
under the weight of snow

and i think of you

i measure my months
by your heartbeat
and match my minutes
with the cadence of your breathing

if anyone ever asks
what my favorite season is
my reply will always be you
wearing summer in your hair
and springtime on your skin

like all things
vast and beautiful
i want to know the depths
of which you exist

it has never been enough
to wade in the shallows

WHY WE'VE COME TO BREAK UNEVENLY

i just want to pack up
and move away
somewhere new

where my friends
don't live in graves
and their names
aren't on the headstones
that fill up the cemeteries

my father

with hands like seasons
held my mother
the night i was conceived

my father

with hands like seasons
hit my mother
as she was creating me

my father

with hands like seasons
held me tightly
the day i was born

my father

with hands like seasons
has stories
scarring his knuckles
about everyone
he's ever loved

my father taught me how to walk when i was two

      - out front doors without looking back
      - away from family you promised forevers to
      - toward dreams that will never be reached

my father taught me forgiveness
is a handshake made in silence

taught me that i'm sorry
will only echo through the past
if the absence is still present

my father taught me how to be a good man
by making sure he was never around

subtracting negatives is how i became the positive

when i was young
my father was statically charged
a violent strike
on quiet nights

i thought,

      "my father is man-made lightning"

i thought,

      "that is why our home is in ruins
        why the foundation is fractured
        and the walls are cracked pine
        and splintered cedar
        why the roof gives way
        to crying skies"

i thought,

      "i am his echo

char
and ash

      against naked earth"

when i grow up
i am going to name my dog yesterday
and plant four o'clocks in my garden
and paint my door california yellow
and tell my neighbors
they are always welcome over for some tea

when i grow up
i will not have the voice of my father
a thunderstorm through cracked wind
i will not have his addictions
his heavy hands and violent ways
nor his knack for leaving everything behind

when i grow up
i know my words will be honey spun
soft edged and sickly sweet
they will not show i am more
vinegar and whiskey
than i am gentle and delicate
and all the things i pretend to be

when i grow up
i will speak my songs into cracked winds
because if i am my father
i will at least provide the chorus
when i become the thunderstorm

this is the best way i can remember it—

there was the color green and i was counting
two by two to all the ways you abandoned me

i got to thirty-three before i realized the
math was wrong and there was no proper way
to add up all the times you fell out of love with me
when i was two years too old to abandon in a womb

i still taste the whiskey you left in my blood
it sits on the backside of my molars
cold and fading
like the footprints left
across my mother's heart
when you walked out

i have learned to take my shoes off and tread lightly
but i need to know there are people like me
who dream of wolves at their throat
have hollowed out the rotten parts
growing inside of themselves
only to find a reflection of the creased skin
they never felt comfortable enough to call their own

the lightning cried
the shoreline swelled
and waters receded
peeling away layers
of the earth's skin

it was like any other day
when your heart stopped
and your life slipped away

the saguaros shrink and
        swell and
this desert town just doesn't feel the same
without you traveling across her skin

i am not lost on the idea
that i am lost without you
and lost on nights where
everything is everywhere and
remembering that you were everything
when you were still here

and lately i've been writing about

        storm clouds
        and flash floods
      gilded flickers
      and violet-streaked chicories

and approximately where the moon was
as the sun set september 26th and
i heard your laughter in the lungs of a child

i want to know when the cities collapse
and the roads fold up like old maps
that we will be together again

the day that john died i could hear the lightning strikes
        the clouds cry
        the mourning doves sing
and the earth split open for him to come home

i remember the thousand suns that lit a fire in the sky
and all the neurons firing at once telling me
to stand
                or sit
                        or fall
as i made my way to my knees

i felt a symphony of teeth crawl through my throat
i thought if i never let his name leave my mouth
then he would never leave this earth

there are days i wake up and all i hear is his laughter
and nights i fall asleep without recognizing my own
times i find a boy wearing his freckles
and hear his voice in a stranger's hello

and i always see his green eyes
staring back at me
through my own

on days when the silence comes
i whisper his name until it turns into a scream
hoping it will drive out the ghosts still stuck in my lungs

it's been four years and i am still holding
his memories in my white-knuckle fists

when do i finally let go of all the anger
let him slip through all the parts of me that remain broken?

john,

sometimes
i feel the sutures i used to sew you up inside of me
pull loose from my wounds
spilling all our old memories out around my feet

sometimes
i feel the body you abandoned and orphaned
crawl up through my stomach
your hands clawing at my lungs
fist pushing out my throat

sometimes
it is so much that i cannot breathe
cannot get the alcohol down to drown you out

john,

my feet have become familiar friends with these streets
every step is one i consciously take to separate myself from the day
i buried you in my past
there's times i don't move at all because the burden i bear becomes
too much
wondering how far i can safely travel without forgetting you
the stillness reminds me how selfish it is to live a life without you
here

john,

the night that you died i held you in my arms and said my goodbyes
i watched you walk away toward the home where you would let
heroin take your life

john,

i wish i would have killed you then
so i would only have to carry around the guilt of taking your life
instead of the guilt i have for not saving it

they say that bad things come in threes so
i am writing about steeping tea
               metaphysics
               and the two billion heartbeats
you left behind

and i am writing a poem about the night you died

i am writing a poem about the night you died
and how you sat in my passenger seat
punching in numbers asking rhetorically to lonely rings
"are there any bridges i haven't burned?"

i still hear your voice echo in the underpass

i still speak to the silence
like it won't last

i am writing a poem about the night you died
and the conversation we had
driving to nowhere because nowhere
was the only place you ever wanted to go

i am writing a poem about
your orphaned bones
my amputated emotions
and how i pretend to feel nothing

and i am writing a poem about the night you died

it's been three years since you passed
and i still count the mourning doves
and the storm clouds
and the lightning strikes

i know they all belong to you now

it's not fair to say i miss you, i know that
to say i miss the violence in your eyes
or the emptiness that came to separate us
i know by the way the sky cracks and cries
you miss infinitely more than i am capable

but still, i do
i miss you

i'm sorry i let the best parts of you
rot away and die inside of me
i'm sorry i was never there to catch you
i'm sorry "goodbye" was the only thing
we never got to say

i'm sorry

i still look for you in the shades of whiskey
still search for you in every autumn breath
still find you in the creases of these old pictures
corners worn thin between my fingertips

i still feel you
in every goddamn corner of this dusty dying town
in every half draw and first choke of a cigarette
in every cold tile step through this house at 3 a.m.

i still feel you
everywhere

i want whatever you took when you left
to return and die inside of me
so i no longer have to look
for the skeletons of our memories
scattered across this state

so i no longer have to name every
            park bench
                                    alleyway
and intersection

after you

so all the coffee shops
and our old haunts
can belong to someone else

so i don't have to hear you singing
from the empty passenger seat
on these quiet car rides home

so i can finally let go of something
that never even belonged to me

i want to say this is the last letter i will ever write to you
that this is the last time i will fall asleep whispering your name
i want to say i have learned to grow straight and strong without
you
that i am not a tangle of knotted limbs and a crooked trunk
trying to grow around the void you left behind
i want to say that i hate you for not loving this life enough
to let me know that you were letting go
i want to hug you and hear your laughter
and fight you and yell at you
for every fucking thing we have all gone through since you
passed away

but i can't

i know you miss us
i know you hear me curse your name every time
a freckle-faced green-eyed child passes by
the weight of his sins not yet soaked into his skin
the burden of blame not yet tied off to his feet
dropped like anchors in the violent waves brewing in his belly
i know you hang your head on nights i am resigned to drink alone
three shots of whiskey for every two that you would consume
because you never quite grew into your frame

and i know you harbor regret

i hear it in the mourning dove's lonely call
in the lightning strikes and the thunder's clap
i know it's not fair to say i miss you
when you miss more than i could ever possibly know

i know

but that is not all i know
i know since you left i have found you in the most unusual places
i still feel you in the silence of every morning
nestling into the settling sighs of this home because
you know today is going to be a long one
i hear you when the songs skip and the static sounds
a collection of voices all speaking at once
every word you never got to live out
and i see you when the alcohol takes hold
the ground spins and i begin to black out
you're just a blur of a boy running scared
from the man you'd grow up and become

and i know this won't be the last letter i write to you

i opened a wound in the earth
        to tuck you away

and as the soil filled around you
covering the last of my dreams

i asked the roots
        and the rocks
        and the oceans
        and the sea

to collapse around me
so i could lay by your side
        one last time

so here it is, growing up. white picket fences feel more
like dividing lines in our family ties than they do a clearly
defined parameter of the lives we have built. matchstick
construction, smoldering cemeteries set to flames by empty
bottles and unfamiliar bedrooms.

i did not sign up for this, the new american dream of broken
hearts and broken homes, a hollow house echoing your
goodbyes. all this time i've been saying i miss you to the
ghost you left behind, cold fingers pressed to the linoleum
where i sleep at night, shoulder blades pressed to an
entryway that has no chance of seeing your return.

and i've still got blueprints beneath my bedsprings titled
"my big plans." an architect and an engineer, i could not
construct a new life with the materials left to me, the son of
a child, the bastard of a lion man.

so there it is, growing up. drawing plot lines and driving
picket posts to keep out the life i so desperately wish to
lead. an empty armed ruler to a kingdom in ruins, my hands
were not equipped to build the structures of support for
those i love the most.

A SONG FOR THOSE LOST AT SEA

i'm so tired
of breathing in
the universe

it only ever
tastes
like you

i thought about
writing a poem explaining
how

      when you are lost at sea
      even if you survive
      you never really come back

then i realized
everyone who's ever been in love
would already understand

i am awake
        she says
i am awake
        she says and i am
remembering sandalwood and petrichor
and the dull scent of gasoline

i am awake and i can feel hands
wrapping around my throat
i am awake and
the cold tile is against my face
and his tobacco-stained teeth are
writing scars into my skin that i cannot erase

i am awake
        i think
i am awake
        i think and it is
because my best friend is dead
i am awake and he is asleep
moon soaked and autumn wrapped
beneath my ribs

i am awake and
i am thinking about how summer feels
and how to calculate the time lost
to accidental death and
how to silence the echoes
from all the things i never said

we are awake and
we share i love you and good night
and we are still
        silent bodies
umbilical tied to people
that were made from mortar shells

we are awake and
we cannot pick the shrapnel from our skin

and i have been
waiting for the devil
living inside of me
to stop making love
to all the ghosts
you left behind

listen

> the promises of
> yesterday's tomorrow are
> only good today

listen

> i felt you bending
> and breaking against the tides
> lying in my arms

look

> i'm not much for haikus because
> i'm still counting the syllables of your goodbyes
> and it's hard to say what's real when
> the best parts of you are shelved
> in glass jars above your mantel

look

> just because we are a pair
> does not mean we match

here

> i do not believe
> in falling stars and i do
> not believe in you

you are perennial
waiting for seasons
that never come

it's simple

the sea swelled
the tides rose
and your waves
        washed
               and wore
through my skin
beating against
the backs of my teeth
the first time
you said my name

and now all i can think of
is how everyone else tastes
like salt water and ocean air

i.   in 8 days you will ask me to leave
       and in 4 years you won't remember my name
       this october i will write
       i am 28 and who is to plan my funeral?
       a line that i never have an answer to

       did you hear the electricity when the lightning struck?
       did you feel yourself move 6 years in the past?

ii.   this is a place we have been before
       standing motionless in the mirror
       wearing lighter hair and softer skins

       what do the wrinkles say?
       that i have waged wars with myself
       only to have lost?

       there are not enough years to undo
       the hatred i have carried
       for every single step

iv.   i don't know about space-time or special relativity
       or why if we travel at
       185,070 miles per second for ten years
       and return back to where we started
       everyone we ever knew would be dead

       i don't understand paper napkin theories
       or infinitely expanding space
       and how it is possible for that
       to be contained to a finite frame

viii. in writing the time traveler's guide
       to planning funerals there is a special section
       dedicated to collecting all the years lost
       spent wishing we were someone else

we compare
one another

to suns
        and moons

name our

sons and daughters

after months
        and seasons

and still we wonder
why people
        come
        and go

i hope you still taste like my love
when the next man kisses you
i hope he feels it in his molars
and it runs down his throat

i hope he knows that you were mine
that you had forevers on your lips
that were only meant for me

i hope he feels small
when he takes hold of your hand
that his fingers will never fill the void
mine have left behind

and when he lays by your side
and whispers that he loves you
i hope my voice echoes back louder
through the canyons i spent nights
carving in the folds of your sheets

i know i have a heart—

it aches every night
i whisper your name
and reach for you
in the empty sheets
lying beside me

i woke up this morning and

washed my face
brushed my teeth
rinsed my mouth

i could still smell you
your scent on my skin
i could still see you
reflecting in my mirror
i could still taste you
between the gap of my lips
to the back of my molars

i woke up this morning and

i could still feel you

      everywhere
      in everything

of course it's you
it's always been you
and how could it not?

i only find you
everywhere
in everything

THE WAYS WE FALL ASLEEP

we live in fear
of silence
because it is filled
with the echoes
of all the things
we left unsaid

sometimes i am drowning

sometimes i am
a throat full of gravel and
                    sand
                            and

cedar-splintered ribs nesting
at the bottom of my belly
and

sometimes i am
waterlogged bones and
eel-snaked limbs and
a head full of violent storms
and

sometimes
i am lying in a bed next to you
formed to a body not my own
and you are a sea
i am ill-equipped to navigate
and

sometimes i pull you close
pray you are my anchor
sometimes your skin
is salt water
and ocean air
and

sometimes i am drowning

she asked me

what's life like
at the bottom
of the sea?

it's hoping
every day
you'll rise
to the surface

i replied

and this is it
this is all we are
just little echoes
fading memories
remembered in fractions
and fragments
moving pictures without sound
just translucent ethereal beings
speaking softly
a delicate voice
against the violent storm

bury me in the soft folds of earth
but do not make time
to visit my remains

know that i am no longer there

i am ivory boned and pulpous marrow
collagen
fiber
and flesh
deconstructed into the elements

i am the blades of grass
pushed between toes
the wild oak
and knotted pine

i am carried in the southern rains
the tepid tides against foreign shores

when i have died
i ask that you bury me
but please do not visit me

i am no longer there

travel across land and sea
on trails not taken
borders not crossed

that is where you will find me

i always knew
what i had to say
would last

i just never knew
my time to say it
would run out
so fast

this is not a poem, but rather an apology for all the ways i have failed as a man. please know there are nights i have slept with my demons and days i have woken up driving out the darkness in hopes that what light is left inside of me could shine for you through all the fractures i forgot to cover in false bravado. i am ready to wear my scars proudly, to demonstrate that i am fully aware of all the times i have gotten it wrong. if you can, forgive me for my sharp edges. it has been harder than i imagined to round out the rough parts, but i am trying.

know that it has taken me 26 years to stop hating myself and i am certain there's still a ways to go. i am aware that i am calloused, worn, rusted, and bruised in all the parts of me that used to shine. but i still care. my god, i care. and i am trying. i just don't have much experience in handling the love another person has to give, to hold the human heart like pressed petals in my palms, tempering the violence that wages inside of me.

there's nights where i find my grace and accept that i no longer need to hate myself. i am trying, please know i am trying, to stay in that moment a little longer for you. it has not been easy to swallow the stones and look on with clear eyes as the sun devours the darkest places i have called home. i know i need it, though, just like i know i need you. accept these dirty palms and gravel-filled knees as a sign that i am finally ready to bleed at your feet all the beauty i have let die inside of me out of fear that one day someone may actually look down at me and say, "you? oh, you are enough and you always have been."

the most difficult
confession
i have ever made
was standing alone
in front of the mirror
telling myself—

"i'm sorry
 i do not love you
 anymore"

after all these years
i've become exhausted
carrying around this much
hatred and anger

my hands have gotten so full
that i'm no longer able
to hold on to the people
i know and love

they've all just slipped away

some nights
the silence is stagnant water
i spend my minutes

wading
          waiting

until it retreats

some nights
the static sounds
grow so loud
the water crowds my throat
and fills my lungs

every night
i experience
some form of drowning

no matter how depression comes
be it in gentle wakes
or violent waves
when the waters rise
it all feels the same

here is how i best understand it—

split the earth in two
cutting carefully
through the equator
then divide them by 360 degrees
and each degree by 60 minutes
every minute along the arc of the earth
is one nautical mile

                              now

circle my circumference
cut me into cross sections
and measure out my miles

                              tell me

how long do we have
before the storm inside of me
swallows us both?

when i was 26, i thought about taking my life a record number of times. i set the highest score for the newest low a human spirit could go, and never once thought about the impact it would have if i went missing from my own life.

that same year, i carved my name into each one of the vertebrae in my best friend's spine. i held her so tightly, all the years i let rot inside of me bled out into her skin. my tears found home in the hollows of her cheeks. some nights, i stay up wondering if anything beautiful ever grew from it all.

when i was 26, there wasn't anything i couldn't do. i didn't yet suffer from brittle bone syndrome and i knew i could shoulder the load that folded up lesser men. i painted light into the darkest corners of my oldest wounds, and changed the trajectory of falling stars simply because i could.

then one morning, i drank enough whiskey to fill my lungs and i could taste the regret my father had when i was born pushing up between my teeth. i pulled weeds from my ribs and picked away the decay that developed in my hands. when the ambulance came, i thought the lights were angels guiding me home. i thought the life i lived was just a dream i was slow to wake from.

so here i am, 26. i've never known how to handle the pain that grows inside of me, but i've learned people are not gardens, and leaving it beneath the welcome mat of their hearts is not an adequate solution anymore. i've pushed everyone away in hopes one of them will fly, but so far the only thing i've ever learned is that we all fall. every time.

over time
i became acutely aware
of what depression really was

the unfortunate occurrence
in which i experienced
my own death
every night

only to wake up
still alive

i just plan on drinking
until i am turpentine and
                    gasoline
until the paint cracks and
                    chips and
strips from my whale bone limbs
and the moonlight covers me in
all the colors i wore
the first time you called me beautiful

i just plan on drinking
until i peel away my skin and
find the version of myself
that you thought you loved

when the lights turn low
i just want to know
that the glow you possess
will be enough
to guide me home

i know my bones
are too heavy
but that doesn't stop me
from staring up
at empty skies
and letting the clouds
consume me

i understand depression
      as the shoreline
      understands the sea

knowing it will retreat
knowing it will recede
knowing it will come

      first in gentle wakes
      then in violent waves
to swallow me
completely

when i was lost at sea
when the waves took hold
and my mind was drowning
you were there to rescue me

and through all of this
the tired
              aching
              weariness
that has settled into our bones
the distance we have traveled
in leaving who we were
to find ourselves again
know that it was you
it was always you
i loved all along

even through the times
you did not love yourself

SONGS MY DAUGHTER WOULD HAVE SUNG

my daughter is a ghost
she is a name my tongue
has forgotten how to speak
she is a song i no longer
remember how to sing

i left a memory
inside the womb of a woman
i did not know how to love

i live with her ghost
i wonder if she still
remembers my name
i wonder if our silence
feels the same

i forgot to tell her
hope is a homemade weapon
i never learned how to wield

i do not know if i ever said sorry
i do not know if i ever learned
the language of forgiveness
or how to touch without
suffocating those i love

. . . and what is this?

a moon being born in your belly?
a stillborn scintilla stuck in your womb?

this is heartache that does not heal

> to plant a seed and
> watch the storm
> carry it away

to let our love
go unnamed

tell me
who held your stars
on nights you forgot how to dream?

who held the notes
when you did not want to sing?

i am sorry

i am sorry

i am sorry i was not the one

my daughter is a cocoon wrapped and

        static limbed
  comatose

cradled in a gossamer womb

on nights i hear her footsteps
a slow traipse through the hallway
i temper my breathing
to match cadence
until we are both

        syncope
     and stopped lungs

for six years i have
tied off i love you's to her name
balloons filled with
        empty echoes

an orphaned frame

i fall asleep
and the sunlight rests
beneath my feet

a black wolf visits
me in my dreams

our daughter is a moon
we cannot console
cradled
   crying
hidden in each horizon

a black wolf walks
beside me in my dreams
my daughter's teeth
sink into my throat

she is a shadow i still hold
an echo crying inside my lungs

i like to think of
how it would have been
had we ever met

on my knees i ask forgiveness
for the man that i still am

i have dreams
where my daughter is
beside the barre

       tendu
       dégagé
       plié

her eyes are
       gouache
           and gold leaf

adagio
allegro
chassé
brisé

she smiles like the bolshoi theatre
alina somova dancing tchaikovsky's *swan lake*

her laughter is danse hongroise, act iii

the curtains rise
a violin bows
i hear her say my name
and the ballet begins

she lives in a rabbit hole and
i visit her on tuesday mornings
we share our common divide
over odd numbers
and how the sun hurts our eyes
but we can never look away

i tell her about the time
my daisies grew rose petals
and tawny tepals and
the four o'clock fields
were faded fuchsia
and heather hues
she tells me she is
contemplating the color purple
and what would be appropriate
to say when she can finally speak
to the flowers
and trees
and saucer-eyed frogs
when she enters their kingdom

i have seen the face of god
she is a four-year-old girl
with questions i have no answers to
and a princess tiara
sitting on the nightstand beside the bed
where she dreams her dreams
every night

it would have been your eighth birthday
we would have sat around drinking from
teacups and you would have told me about
the primrose garden you had planted
with your mother the day before

we would have run through sprinklers
lit the candles that you can't blow out
and chased minnows in the creek

we would have sung "happy birthday"
with you on my lap
bright eyed and raven haired
teeth too large and a smile
that framed them just right

i still blow up the balloons
and order the cake
i still sit in silence
and call out your name

when you feel your life fading
do not fear
        little human
death has not come to take you

        rather

she is making you brand new

back you will go
        to the stars that bore you
back to the winds
        that carried your first
        and last
breath

back to the soils
        that harvested your life
back you will go
little human

back to where your life began

do not grow old; that is foolish. collect the lessons life gives and file them under "things i have learned," but do not ever let them age you, my dear. time is not a death march, it is just an easy way to index the exact moments you left your mark on another life.

you have 60 minutes to an hour and 24 hours to a day so give away smiles freely, over compliment, and love entirely.

always keep the sunshine on your skin, the warmth of your voice, and the glow in your eye. what created the stars also created you. do not ever doubt that you burn just as brightly.

you will be hurt, broken, and ripped open. remember back to your first ride without training wheels when we learned that everything heals, and the scars are just times you colored outside the lines of the magnificent creation that you are.

people will come like scars. not to say "this is where you have been hurt," but to help you patch yourself together again. let them.

when you were born there were thunderstorms as you cried and the earth shook when you laughed. you have always been a force of nature. there is no reason anyone or anything should ever make you feel small.

lastly, on days you feel you are not enough, always remember the first man who ever said he loved you will always mean it, and the first woman to kiss you did so unconditionally. they will always accept what you choose to be, and will always be your shield and support, your shoulder to cry on, and ear to confide in.

IN YOUR ATTIC, UNDER THE STARS

the only parts of sunshine
that i will ever need
are the parts that shine down
over you and me

the foundation split and
your heart divided into
so many pieces tethered off to
so many faces and so many places
searching for someone and something
you could call your own

how long has it been
since you found steady footing?
how many men have come before
pocket full of promises
weighted words you wished were real?

though they were hollow
i can still feel them as i hold you
heavy against your heart

i will show you calloused hands
and bloody knuckles
and aching muscles

it has not been easy
building a place inside myself
that you could call home

but if you give me your heart
i will show you how forever feels
and over time
the place where we reside
will come to be defined
as the empty space between fingers
the creases of just-kissed lips
and the hollows of each other's arms

you will always be
where i return
and i
i will always be
who you call home

one day i will kiss you
kiss you with lips that understand
kiss you with lips that can better explain
that can speak in so many languages

they will know how to say i love you
in ways you have never heard
in ways that sound unlike anything
any other man has mouthed before
false promises and fairy tales
they did not ever believe in

one day i will kiss you
pressed words between your lips
i will kiss you and they will
rattle between your teeth
run down your throat
and fill your lungs
they will echo against your ribs
they will reverberate through your limbs
they will dress every corner
you've kept sadness hidden away
until all that grows inside of you
is the understanding that you are enough

one day i will tell you all about
my paper napkin theories
algorithms i formed that demonstrate
how the sum of all that you are
is greater than infinity
but to me you have always been the one

in all the wishes that i made
as i dreamed my dreams
last night

the only wish i wished came true
is the wish that i woke up
right next to you

out of all the
how we mets
i've had to tell
ours will always be
my favorite

tell me your secrets
and i will show you mine
tell me about your
glass bottle wishes
and i will show you
the shipwreck graveyards
where my dreams go to die

tell me about
the distance you have traveled
in order to find yourself
and i will show you the depths
in which you exist

        leagues
        and echoes

you alone are greater than

        the oceans
        and seas

from which we came

wherever the world goes
when you close your eyes
that's where i want to be
as long as you are by my side

you be
the clouds above
i'll be
the grass below
and everything
in between
will be where
our love will grow

it is perhaps
my greatest fear
that when we
no longer exist
in these bodies
i will not be able
to find you again

we've all fallen
been mistreated
and handled
too roughly

but through all
the cracks
and brokenness
we possess a glow
that outshines
everything

the most beautiful thing
we are capable of doing
is not opening ourselves
to let another person in

it's picking up the pieces
and putting ourselves
back together
after they leave

ready to greet the next
one with open arms

love is not the absence of hate
hate will always exist

love is holding our head high
and forever moving forward
with kindness and compassion
in spite of what hate may bring

because no amount of darkness
can drown out our light
if our light has been lit within

i am sorry for the burdens i bear
and the crosses i must carry
and the path i have chosen

it is not flesh and bone
that weighs me down, my dear
i speak to you gently
and care for you infinitely
but if ever i am silent
do not ask if i am okay

i am not okay

there are wars being waged inside of me
fights in the darkness against demons
whose names i do not know

if i speak too softly
it is because i do not wish to wake them
if i touch you too gently
it is because i feel their claws coming out of me
and if i let you lead
it is because i fear where they will take me

please forgive me for the times i fail
but understand i am trying
it has not been easy learning to handle
a heart like yours

you are all things sweet and pure
as lovely as any one human can be
and i do not ever want my darkness
to stain your brilliant light

but if you tell me
you don't mind the scars
i will touch you with everything i am
and if you tell me you are not afraid
i will take you by the hand
i will take you through my darkness
i will show you where your light
has always shined the brightest

you are so much sunlight
smiling through
such a small frame

dandelions dance
against the horizon
the sun lies across
the contours of your chest
shadows hide
in the recesses of your clavicle
the moon melts over your skin

i've charted every inch
the peaks
                    and valleys
of your spine

the lulls of your ribs
and the crest of your hips

i've found the
bay area shoreline
the arizona desert
and the northern pines

every freckle a mile marker
every scar a point to plot
your body is an adventure
waiting to be written

she was the greatest force of all
because she never chose to destroy

instead

she went off into darkness
seeking out the demons
and those cast aside

not to drive them away
but rather

to show them that even they
were capable of creating
the most unimaginable light

the one person we have to talk to
every single day

no matter
          the time
          the circumstance
or place

is ourselves

will you reply with kindness
and sympathy
when the days become difficult?

will you share in the joy
and celebration
as you accomplish your dreams?

always be aware
of how you speak to yourself
every word is heard loudly
even if said in the silence
of your mind

this morning
the stars folded into the moon
sunk off in the horizon
and the sun rose
just for you

so if you ever feel alone
or doubt your worth
remember one thing

galaxies have shifted
just for the chance
to see you shine

so shine

i can't say i know
the burdens you bear
the struggles you face
or the fights you have fought
in learning to love yourself

i do not have the answers
                    the solutions
                    or remedies
you may be searching for

but i do have something
and though it's just one thing
i will give you all that i can

and through my kindness
i hope you will start to see
that you alone are enough
you alone have always been
and you alone will always be

just that
                    enough

for everyone
for everything

come to me
        wild and untamed

bring the oceans on your lips
the mountains on your spine
i want to explore all the places
you have ever called home

let me pluck each petal
from the gardens you've grown
overcrowded seedlings
pushing up through your bones

come to me
        dipped in the stars
come to me
        wearing all your scars

i want to show you
just how beautiful you are

you are not poetry
you are not something
that can be summed up

      in words

rather

you are all things beautiful
only seen through the actions
of a pure and perfect heart

i don't ever want to look at you
and have to say,

       "she's the one that got away"

i want you to be able to look at me
and know i'm the one who got it right
i want to be the one that stays

my favorite sound
is that of your name
as i whisper it softly
against the small of your neck
each and every morning
before you pull me close
hands to hips
and start the day
        sigh
                tremble
and soft moan
exhaling the dreams you had
down the back of my throat

in every word i speak
i leave the best parts of you
littered across these streets

love is knowing
every goodbye
has a hello
on the horizon

they ask me how i love you
and i say in pages
            in novels
            in volumes

i love you like my favorite story
the one that i wake up to
every day
and watch unfold

and i don't know how it ends
but i know your name
is already written
in the chapters of my life
that i have yet to live

happiness
is a heartbeat

home
is a pair of hands
to hold

and of all the things
i look forward to in life
falling in love with you
is at the top of the list

the way the sun
chases the moon
i will always chase you

you are the daydream
i am supposed to have
for the rest of my life

i know the sun rises in the east
and sets in the west

that i am ten fingers
            and ten toes
            and ten thousand
reasons short of explaining
what it is i can't explain to you

and i know
that i will always love you

            in certainties

may the sweet scent
hidden in these sheets
always belong to you

and the first breath
pulled from my chest
carry your name

above all else
i would choose you

when there's no more
grand gestures
no more words to say
when everything around us
begins to give way
when the sky grows dim
and the colors fade

i will choose you

do not let your lips leave mine again

it is without permission i have glued my fingertips
to the parts of yourself that you have found to be unworthy
i will teach you that your flaws are not flaws
they are just bruises and scars and misplaced parts
that don't make sense and don't really matter
because you're still someone
and that's something
especially in a world that is so full of nothing

i will go slow and handle you gently
cradle your bones in the creases of my palms
and teach you how to appreciate art

but you must not let your lips leave mine again
because the last time they did the stars all rusted
the sun stopped spinning
and the moon broke down
the clouds dropped from the sky
the winds quit blowing
birds quit chirping
and the ocean swallowed up the shoreline

so don't ever let your lips leave mine
unless it is to whisper, "kiss me again"

your mother ate two bowls of cheerios
before bed when you were in her womb

now you are honey nut eyes
and sweet milk skin and
all i can think about in the soft moments
before i sleep is the sound of your laughter
coming from my passenger seat

tell me you have been searching for a home
in every empty promise packaged up
in pretty words from another's mouth
and i will tell you that i know

i tasted their sharp edges when we kissed
pride commands you keep them in
swallow them down
don't let anyone know how much they hurt

tell me about every bruise
about why your heart is black and blue
about every shade and every hue
you have worn from being misused

i'll tell you about french rose
hidden in the arizona sunsets and
amaranth blush pulled from my cheeks

that you're the bravest thing i have ever held
and i've been covering the bruises
in pink pastels and white rose
dressed in peonies

that the colors of heartache
will never show through
these coats of love

*hello, little bird
you mean the sunshine to me
the moon chirped to her*

Andrews McMeel Publishing
a division of Andrews McMeel Universal
1130 Walnut Street, Kansas City, Missouri 64106

www.andrewsmcmeel.com

17 18 19 20 21 BVG 10 9 8 7 6 5 4 3 2 1

ISBN: 978-1-4494-8650-1

Library of Congress Control Number: 2017940144

Editor: Patty Rice
Designer/Art Director: Diane Marsh
Production Editor: David Shaw
Production Manager: Cliff Koehler